Home Guide to Balcony Gardening

For Under £50

By DL Reid

Home Guide to Balcony Gardening

For Under £50

By DL Reid

Contents

Introduction

Dear reader during these unprecedented times we do not always know what tomorrow brings. However, we can rest assured should we take the necessary steps to prepare ourselves for the inevitable.

This book is a guide that will give you basic knowledge and tools on how to grow a fruit or vegetable garden on your balcony for less than fifty pounds (£50). With the use of tools, equipment and reusable gadgets that we take for granted in the home.

This six-step easy guidebook will ensure you are prepared in a more sophisticated way for tomorrow.

I hope you find this useful and wish you the best of luck with your balcony gardening.

Tools and Equipment	**Price**
Greenhouse	£9.16
Starter plant pots	£3.29 *or*
use plastic cups	
Spray bottle	£3.99
Water canister or 5ltr bottle or jug	£2.99
Soil (All purpose)	£10 *for*
10L	
Fruit/Vegetable grow bag 3 gallon	£3.49
Seeds	£2.99
3-piece garden tool	£3.99

These prices are a guide tool that can be purchased on Amazon and or eBay.

Alternately, should you wish to purchase your goods using any other digital marketing platform or enter a shop to purchase, this is totally your choice.

Stages

1. Seedlings

Sort out your seeds and look at what you have. Check on the back of the packet to notify when it is best to plant these seeds. This will give you a good indicator when to start preparing. If you do not have a certain seed you can take what you have in your fridge or pantry and follow the instructions on the next stage '*sprouting*' to help.

2. Sprouting

This is when the seed is germinated. A very simple method is to get a jar and place a clean kitchen hand tissue in the center ensuring that it is pressing against the glass. Add your seeds or beans one at a time on the outside of the tissue leaving a finger width of space in between each. Add a little bit of water to the centre of the jar just enough for the tissue to absorb but not breakdown. Store the jar in a warm dry place and lighted space.

3. **Transfer to cultivate**

Before the transfer you should see that by now the seeds have grown roots and even stems, this means that they are ready. First fill your starter plant pots or egg boxes with soil. Place a finger hole in the soil in the middle of each starter pot. Then carefully transfer your sprouts (roots facing down) into the pot and cover with the soil. ***NB. Be gentle***

Once all your sprouts have been transferred in their pots place then in the greenhouse. Be sure to keep them in a warm environment should you not have a greenhouse and mist with a spray bottle each day to maintain a healthy growth. This is where they will stay until the plant begins to outgrow the starter pots.

When the plants outgrow the starter pots or egg boxes, (which ever you choose to use) they are ready to be placed in the grow bag. Similar to the starter boxes ensure that the bags are filled with soil. You want to ensure there is enough soil in the grow bags so that the roots can grow and the plants can get enough nutrients.

All that is in the starter pots you will transfer to the grow bag. Be sure to continuously label your pots and bags as you might confuse yourself and place a plant into the wrong bag. So again, a little further preparation.

4. **Looking after your plants**

This really is the easiest part so if you have successfully got to this section, you have already come through the hardest part. Continue to water your plants each day using the water canister or jug. Should a day be extremely hot, spray the plants throughout the day to ensure the leaves or plant does not burn or dry out. If there are little unwanted green at the base of the plant, they are just weeds you can pull them right out. This process will continue until harvest.

5. **Harvesting**

Remember at the beginning there were instructions on the back of the seed packets? You may go back to this or simply wait until you are sure your fruit or vegetable is ready for picking.

Some fruits and vegetables will be ready before others and that is alright. Depending on the growth cycle one can get two to three or even six harvests in the same year. This solely depends on the fruit, vegetable or salad crop.

Leafy Greens or Salad

No need to pull out from the soil, using a pair of scissors cut close to the stem and you will later get new sprout.

Hanging Fruits or Vegetables (tomatoes, peppers, plums, lemons)

They will grow all what they can for that year. However, once they are picked they will not grow back until the following year. Therefore, you may decide on planting more so you can store and use throughout the year.

Unearthed Vegetables (potatoes, carrots, onions, garlic)

These bad boys are what rejuvenation is all about; they do not sit around and wait. Given that they are in the right environment (heat, moisture and light) they will start their growing process all over again without soil. However this can be short lived if not transferred to cultivate in time.

These vegetables are unearthed from the soil by using a fork or by simply pulling the stem until they loosen from the earth (soil). They can sit in a dry place for several months. So ensure you have a dry cool place to store them so that they do not spoil so easily.

6. **Storing and Preserving**

Leafy Green or Salad Leaves

As quick as they grow is as quick as they spoil and so, keep them in the fridge or store them in the freezer.

Hanging Fruits & Vegetables

These too can be stored in the fridge however; they can be sustained outside of the fridge. Just ensure that they are kept is cool dry spaces such as; a trolley or fruit bowel, should you want to preserve them then store them in sterilised airtight preserving jars and these can be stored in the pantry or on a shelf.

Unearthed Vegetables

These vegetables are best kept in dry cool places such as; pantries, trolleys, dry air bags or air tight plastic bags.

These are the basic and general steps to gardening from seed to harvest in confined spaces and can be used for larger plots. For example; back gardens and terraces. Using spacing wisely and knowing that one can grow food from the comfort of their home without breaking the bank is a skill that none can take away. So go ahead and share this newfound knowledge with your family and friends and enjoy the fruits of your labour. Even better you can purchase and get the starter kits online.

Vegetable & Fruits

Below lists some fruits and vegetables to grow on the balcony below:

Beans
Beetroot
Bell pepper
Brussels Sprout
Carrots
Celery
Chard
Chilli
Courgette/
Zucchini
Cucumber
Ginger
Herbs
Kale
Lemon
Lettuce
Limes
Onions
Peas
Plums
Potato
Root Vegetables
Spinach
Spring onions
Tomato

Pumpkin Plant

Pumpkin Flower

Pumpkin Flower

Pumpkin, Bean & Potato Leaves

Gratitude

I wish to extend my upmost gratitude and praise to the Almighty God (Allah). Who has provided us with the tools of Mother Nature, who has inspired me and blessed me with a gift I was unaware of having and am now am able to share with other people.

I will like to thank you all who have purchased this book; I pray you find it useful and are able to enjoy the many fruits of your labour.

May God bless you

If you enjoyed this book please purchase
Recycling with Children and *Balcony Composting*
by DL Reid.

Fan mail at: icence973@gmail.com

Printed in Great Britain
by Amazon